Pre-Primer Level

Schaum
Keyboard Alphabet Workbook

For the Very Early Child Beginner
at Piano or Electronic Keyboard
for Private or Class Instruction

Developed by Sue Pennington
Edited by Wesley Schaum

FOREWORD

This workbook is intended for the very young beginner at the keyboard and may be used in private lessons as well as class teaching. It serves as a very helpful supplement to an individualized program or to a method book such as Schaum's Keyboard Talent Hunt, Book 1. The learning concepts and progression are planned for children age 4 to 6.

These workbook pages help save valuable time during the piano lesson, especially in a class situation where they have been developed and tested. They can be used during the lesson and also as homework.

Flash cards are included at the end of the book. They may be left as is, or cut apart along the broken lines. Answers are printed on the back of each card for convenient use at home as well as during the lesson.

Basic Concepts Presented:
- White key letter names
- Finger numbers for both hands
- Five-finger positions (C and G)
- Simple rhythmic relationship of whole, half and quarter notes

TO PARENTS

A small amount of your time spent with your child will greatly increase his/her benefits from this workbook. You do not need to know anything about music! Here are some guidelines:
- The best time to do these workbook assignments is as soon as possible after the lesson, while things are still fresh in your child's mind.
- Know what has been assigned. Contact the teacher if your child is not sure of the assignment.
- Be sure your child understands the directions. Read them through several times, if necessary.
- The workbook should be brought to every lesson for review and new assignments by the teacher.
- Help your child with flash cards, as assigned by the teacher. Answers are on the back of each card.
- Your child may need extra help with writing letters and numbers. Be very patient and go slowly.

Schaum Publications, Inc.

EXCLUSIVELY DISTRIBUTED BY

HAL•LEONARD®
CORPORATION
7777 W. BLUEMOUND RD. P.O. BOX 13819 MILWAUKEE, WI 53213

ISBN-13: 978-1-936098-10-1

02-10

Schaum Keyboard Alphabet Workbook

DIRECTIONS

Teaching very young children can be a real joy, but it requires special patience and a sympathetic understanding of the wide differences in their normal mental and physical development. A pupil at age 4, 5, or 6 simply does not learn as quickly as an older child. Because of the short attention span of a very young child, the teacher should have many learning aids and techniques ready to use to keep the student focused during the lesson.

For maximum benefit, this workbook should be used as part of the homework assignment as well as at the lesson. When a child tires of keyboard work, a workbook page can be started. It is advisable to finish most of the page *at the lesson,* especially when a new concept is presented, or when there is trouble retaining a concept from a previous lesson. Obviously, most children will not be able to read the instructions on each page; therefore it is important that the assignment be understood by the student before leaving the studio.

Pupils at this age vary widely in the rate in which they learn and the amount of material they retain. It is quite normal for very young children to forget (partially or completely) what they have been taught from one week to the next. The ability to remember is something that develops gradually and differs from one child to another. For this reason much repetition and review are included in this book. In some cases, the teacher may need to provide additional help until the learning concepts are firmly grasped by the student.

If the student knows how to write his/her name (even if only the first name), let him/her write it on each workbook page when it is assigned. This is fun for the young child and enhances self esteem.

It is recommended that the child use an *erasable* pen or pencil at first. A pencil with extra-thick lead may be helpful. After a page has been checked by the teacher and corrected by the child (if necessary) a crayon, magic marker, or colored pencil could be used to draw over the original pencil lines for review. If magic marker is used, be sure the ink is *washable* and a type that does not soak through the paper.

Award stickers (such as Schaum's *Musical Award Seals* - catalog #40-07), or colored stars are important for student motivation. Stars of different colors could be used to create a simple grading system. Be sure to use stickers for every lesson (on both sides of each page).

HANDWRITING HINTS

Four and five year olds frequently write slowly and make letters and numbers rather crudely. This is normal because the necessary coordination and muscle control develop gradually at this age. It depends upon the child's physical development and is not necessarily related to age. For some pupils, this book may be their first attempt at writing alphabet letters other than their own name. Extra patience and understanding at the lesson plus help at home may be needed in such cases.

Even if the young child has much difficulty writing letters and numbers, bear in mind that the primary goal should be for the student to *identify* the letters and numbers, and to *corollate* the numbers with the fingers of each hand and the letters with the keys of the keyboard.

Lesson 1

Name _____

Trace each letter on the grey lines.

A A B B C C D D E E F F G G

Trace each letter, then print your own letter beside each tracing.

A   B   C   D   E   F   G

Trace each letter on the keyboard below.

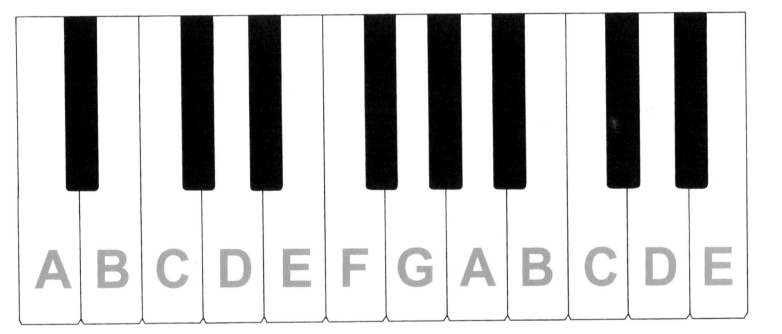

Print each letter on the keyboard below.

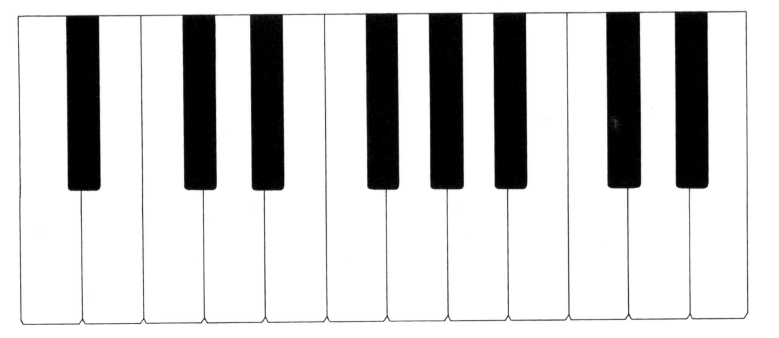

Lesson 2

Name _____

Find and print the letter A (there are two places).   Find and print the letter D (there are two places).

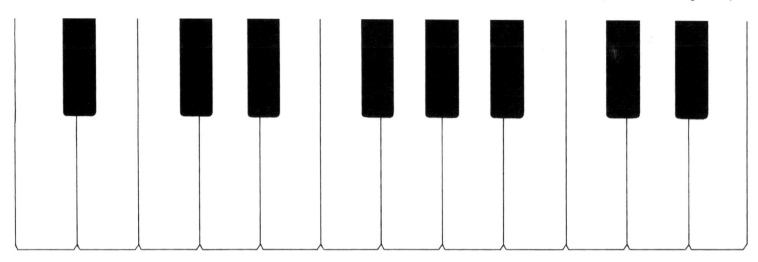

Find and print the letter C (there are two places).   Find and print the letter F (there is one place).

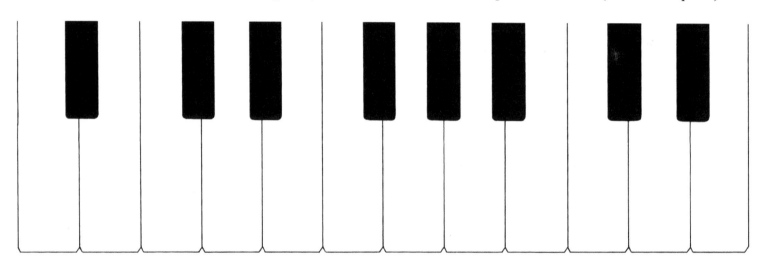

Find and print the letter E (there are two places).   Find and print the letter B (there are two places).

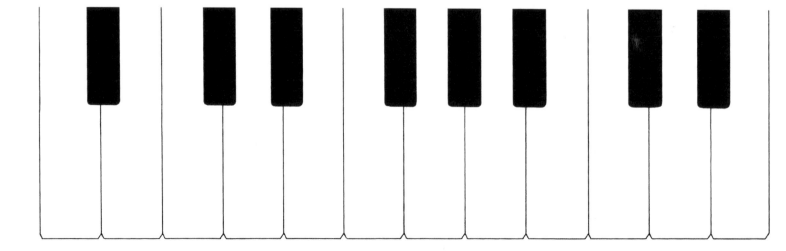

Lesson 3

Name _____

Trace each of the grey numbers below.
Then trace the numbers on each of the fingers.

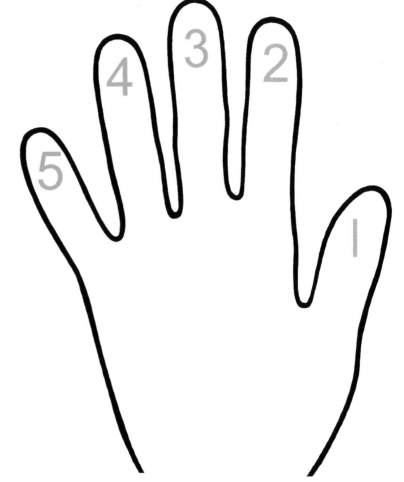

Place your LEFT hand flat in the space below and draw an outline around the fingers and hand.
Then print the correct number on each finger.

Lesson 4

Name _____

Trace each of the grey numbers below.
Then trace the numbers on each of the fingers.

Place your RIGHT hand flat in the space below and draw an outline around the fingers and hand.
Then print the correct number on each finger.

Lesson 5

Name _____

This is a keyboard group with TWO black keys. The white keys in this group are always named C - D - E.

Trace the letter names of the three white keys in this group.

This is a keyboard group with THREE black keys. The white keys in this group are always named F - G - A - B.

Trace the letter names of the four white keys in this group.

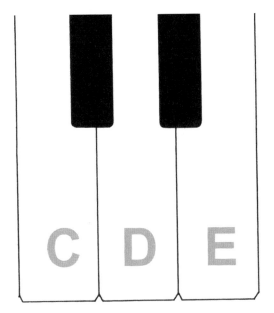

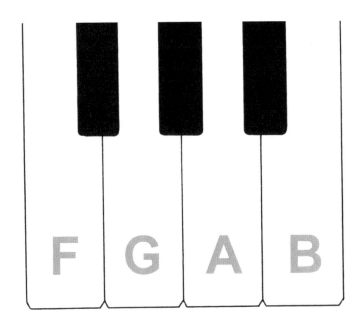

Print the letter names of the three white keys in this group.

Print the letter names of the four white keys in this group.

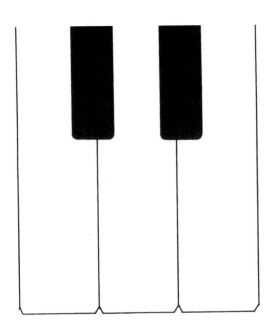

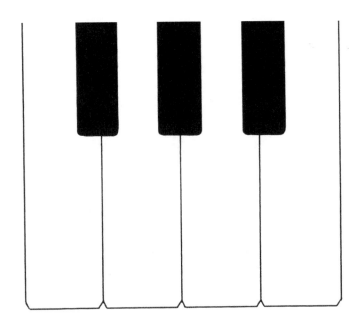

Lesson 6

Name _____

Find and print the letter D.

Find and print the letter A.

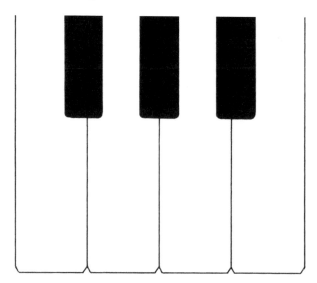

Find and print the letter C.

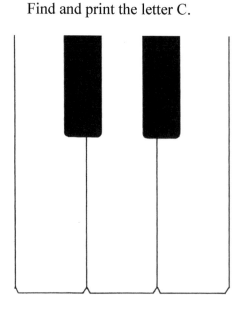

Find and print the letter B.

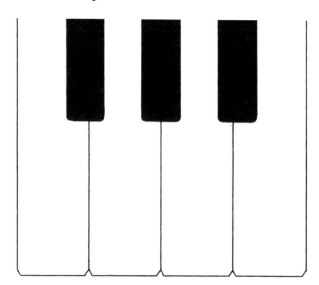

Find and print the letter E.

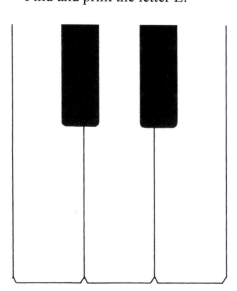

Find and print the letter G.

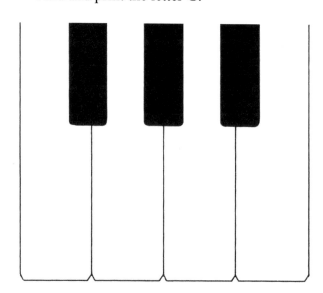

Lesson 7

Name _____

Place your LEFT hand flat on this page, with each finger covering one finger number. With the hand in place, draw an outline around the fingers and hand.

4   3   2

5

|

Place your RIGHT hand flat on this page, with each finger covering one finger number. With the hand in place, draw an outline around the fingers and hand.

2   3   4

5

|

Lesson 8

Name _____

Draw an "X" through any WRONG letters. Then print the CORRECT letter above each wrong one.

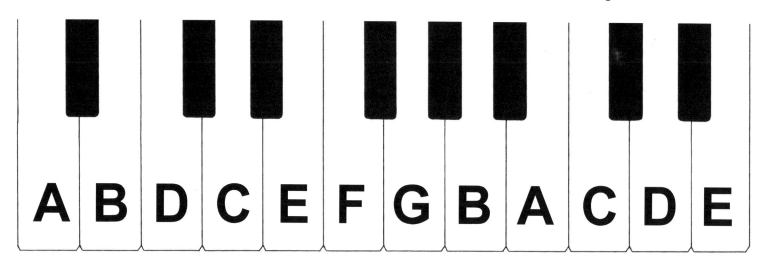

Draw an "X" through any WRONG letters. Then print the CORRECT letter above each wrong one.

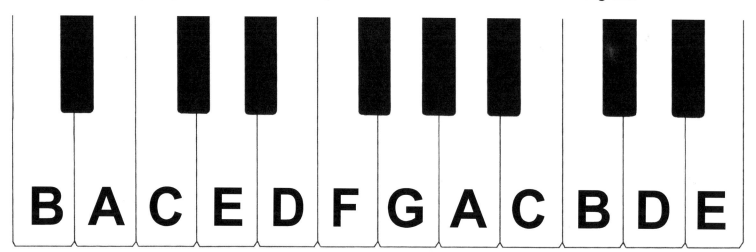

Draw an "X" through any WRONG letters. Then print the CORRECT letter above each wrong one.

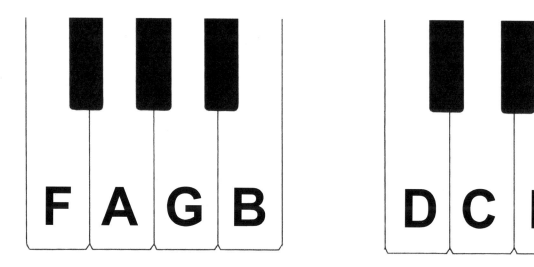

Lesson 9

Draw an "X" through any WRONG finger numbers.
Then print the CORRECT number below the wrong one.

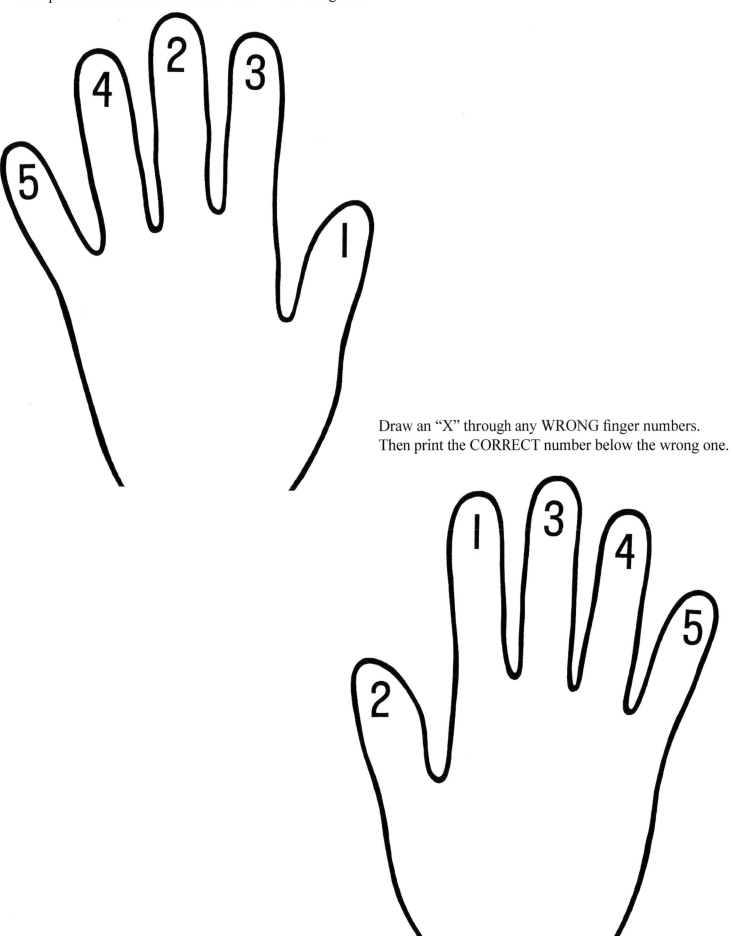

Draw an "X" through any WRONG finger numbers.
Then print the CORRECT number below the wrong one.

Lesson 10

Name _____

Print the missing letters on this keyboard.

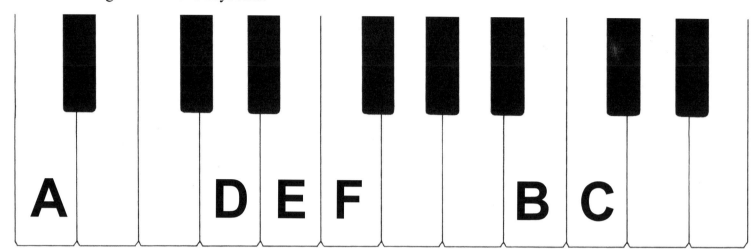

Print the missing letters on this keyboard.

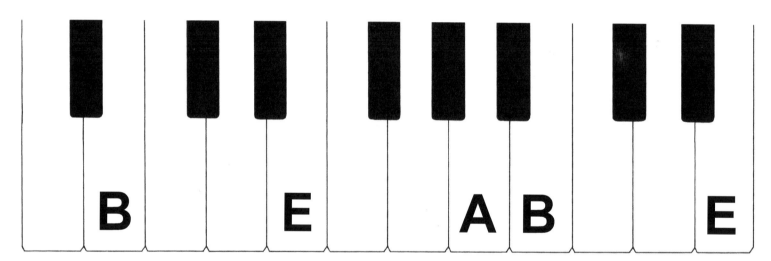

Print the missing letters on this keyboard.

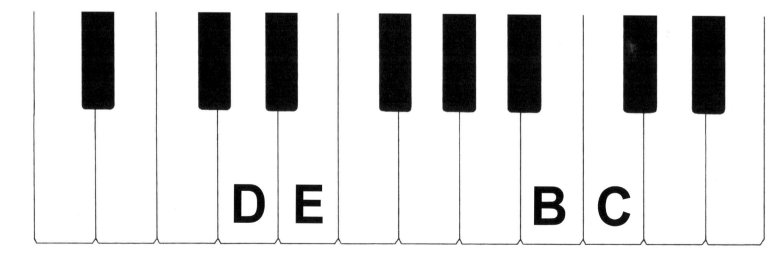

Lesson 11

Name _____

Print the missing letters on this keyboard.

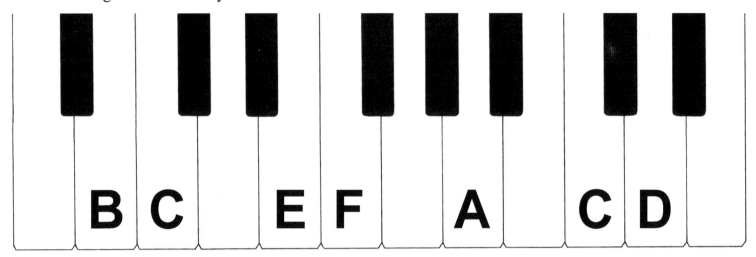

Print the missing letters on this keyboard.

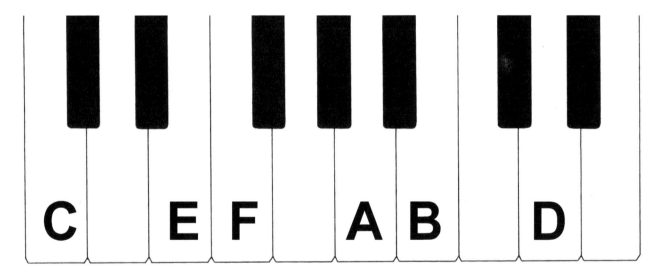

Print the missing letters on this keyboard.

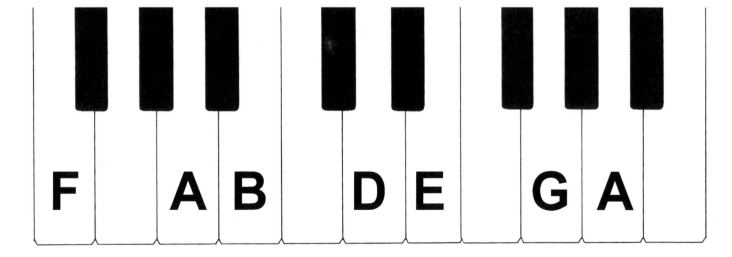

Lesson 12

Name _____

Print the letters of the C Hand Position (C - D - E - F - G) on the white keys.

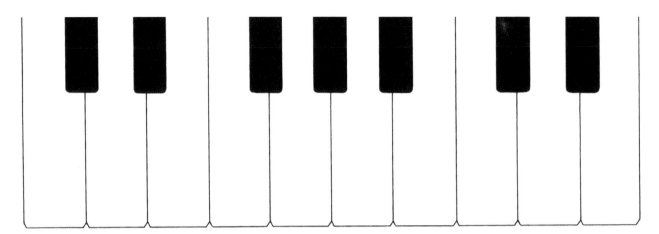

Print the letters of the C Hand Position on each finger of both hands. Then print the correct number above each finger.

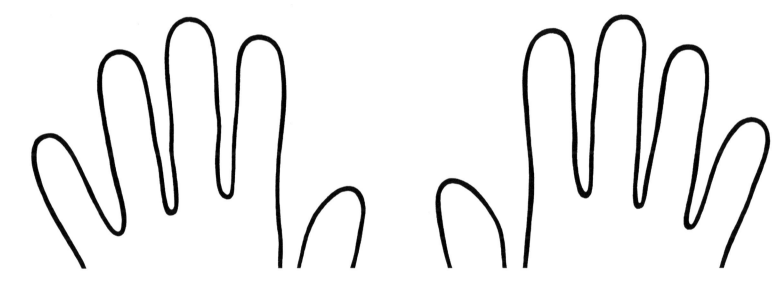

Print the letters of the C Hand Position (C - D - E - F - G) on the white keys.

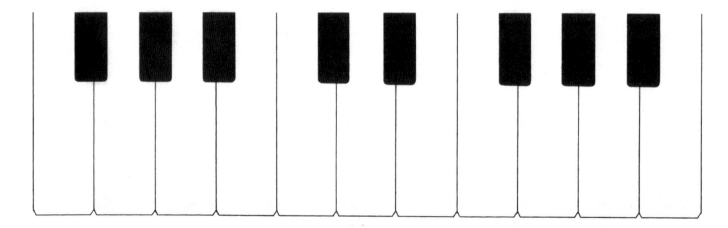

Lesson 13

Name _____

Print the letters of the G Hand Position (G - A - B - C - D) on the white keys.

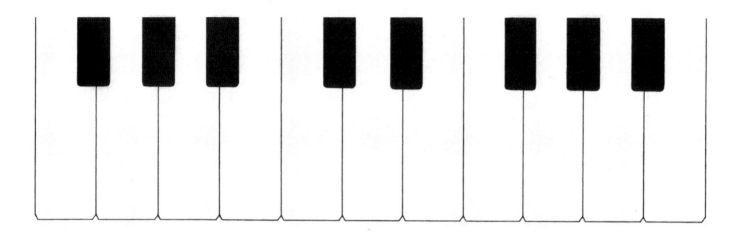

Print the letters of the G Hand Position on each finger of both hands. Then print the correct number above each finger.

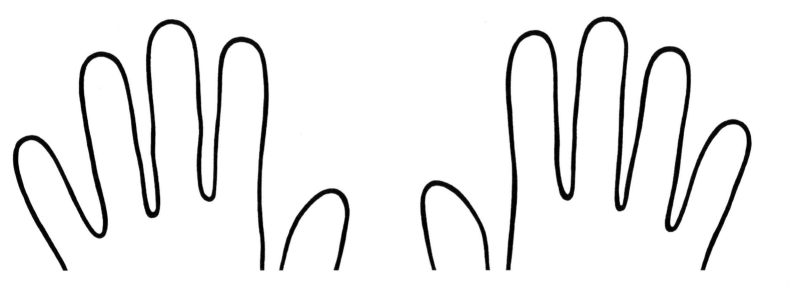

Print the letters of the G Hand Position (G - A - B - C - D) on the white keys.

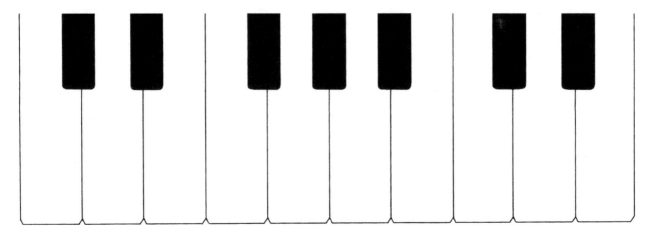

Lesson 14

Name _____

Trace a WHOLE note (see above).	Trace two HALF notes (see above).	Trace four QUARTER notes (see above)
Draw a WHOLE note.	Draw two HALF notes.	Draw four QUARTER notes.
Draw a WHOLE note.	Draw two HALF notes.	Draw four QUARTER notes.

Lesson 15

Name _____

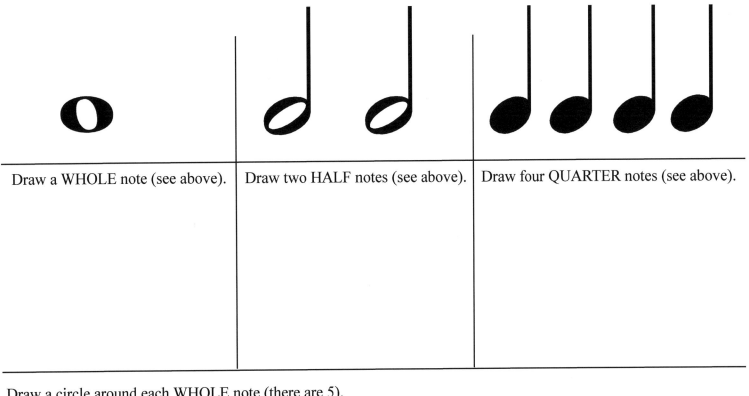

| Draw a WHOLE note (see above). | Draw two HALF notes (see above). | Draw four QUARTER notes (see above). |

Draw a circle around each WHOLE note (there are 5).

Draw a circle around each HALF note (there are 5).

Draw a circle around each QUARTER note (there are 5).

Lesson 16

Name _____

Find and print the letter D.

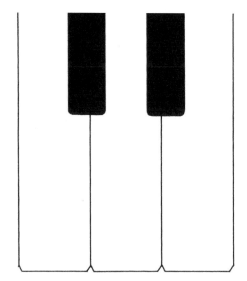

Find and print the letter F.

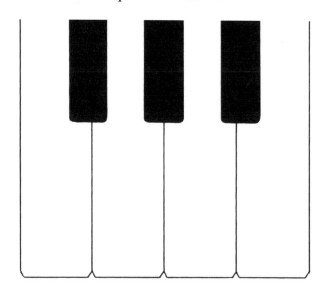

Find and print the letter A.

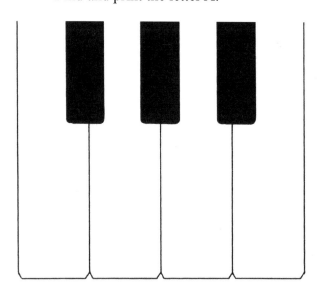

Find and print the letter C.

Find and print the letter E.

Find and print the letter G.

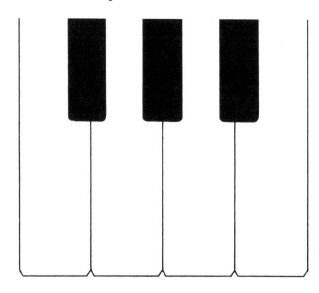

G	D	C
A	RIGHT Hand	E
B	LEFT Hand	F
QUARTER Note	HALF Note	WHOLE Note